Reflections:

Paintings & Poems from a Poet's Gallery

"The only true journey involves seeing the universe with the eyes of another."
—Marcel Proust

"My imagination can picture no fairer happiness than to continue living for art."
—Clara Schumann

Cover image: Our dock at Dunningford Cove, Jack Bay, off the Patuxent River. A number of the poems in this collection were written and rewritten here where artists, poets, writers and musicians gather.

Books and Chapbooks by Elisavietta Ritchie

BABUSHKA'S BEADS: A GEOGRAPHY OF GENES Poets' Choice Publishers (2016)

GUY WIRES Poets' Choice Publishers (2015)

IN HASTE I WRITE YOU THIS NOTE: STORIES & HALF-STORIES
    Washington Writers' Publishing House (e-book 2015)

TIGER UPSTAIRS ON CONNECTICUT AVENUE
    (Cherry Grove Collections, WordTech Communications (2013)

FEATHERS, OR, LOVE ON THE WING
    Shelden Studios, collaboration with artists Megan Richard, Suzanne Shelden (2013)

FROM THE ARTIST'S DEATHBED Winterhawk Press (chapbook 2012)

CORMORANT BEYOND THE COMPOST Cherry Grove Collections (2011)

REAL TOADS Black Buzzard Press (chapbook, 2008)

AWAITING PERMISSION TO LAND Cherry Grove Collections (2006)

THE SPIRIT OF THE WALRUS Bright Hill Press (chapbook 2005)

IN HASTE I WRITE YOU THIS NOTE: STORIES & HALF-STORIES,
    Washington Writers' Publishing House (2000)

THE ARC OF THE STORM Signal Books (1998)

ELEGY FOR THE OTHER WOMAN: NEW & SELECTED POEMS
    Signal Books (1996)

WILD GARLIC: THE JOURNAL OF MARIA X.
    Harper Collins (novella in verse, chapbook 1995)

A WOUND-UP CAT AND OTHER BEDTIME STORIES
    Palmerston Press (chapbook, 1993)

FLYING TIME: STORIES & HALF-STORIES Signal Books (1986, 1988)

THE PROBLEM WITH EDEN Armstrong State College Press, (chapbook 1985)

RAKING THE SNOW Washington Writers' Publishing House (1982)

A SHEATH OF DREAMS & OTHER GAMES Proteus Press (chapbook 1976)

TIGHTENING THE CIRCLE OVER EEL COUNTRY Acropolis Books (1974)

TIMBOT The Lit Press (novella-in-verse, chapbook, 1970)

Poetry Anthologies Edited:

THE DOLPHIN'S ARC: Poems on Endangered Creatures of the Sea
    SCOP (1986)

FINDING THE NAME Wineberry Press (1983)

Reflections:

Paintings & Poems from a Poet's Gallery

ELISAVIETTA RITCHIE

Poets' Choice

Poets' Choice Publishing

Copyright © 2017 Poets' Choice Publishing
All rights reserved
Printed in the United States of America

Consultant work:
www.WilliamMeredithFoundation.org

Bulk discounts available through www.Poets-Choice.com

Cover photo: Elisavietta Ritchie
Author's photo: Clyde H. Farnsworth

Library of Congress Cataloging-in-Publication Data pending
ISBN 978-0-9972629-1-9

Poets' Choice Publishing
337 Kitemaug Road
Uncasville, CT 06382
Poets-Choice.com

REFLECTIONS

For all the artists
forever alive in us.

Table of Contents

- ix   Preface, by Richard Harteis
- xi   Author's Note

- 3   Anonymous: *Cat and Kittens*
- 5   John James Audubon: *Arctic Hare*
- 7   John James Audubon: *Snowy Egret*
- 9   John Woodhouse Audubon: *The Long-Tailed Red Fox*
- 11   Hendrick Avercamp: *A Scene on Ice*
- 13   Adolphe Blondheim: *The Decoration*
- 15   Mary Blumberg: *A Gift of Tomatoes*
- 17   Pierre Bonnard: *Her Children*
- 19   Pierre Bonnard: *The Letter*
- 21   Mary Cassatt: *The Loge*
- 23   Paul Cezanne: *Still Life*
- 25   Paul Cezanne: *Man with Pipe*
- 27   Paul Cezanne: *Pyramid of Skulls*
- 29   Jean Simeon Chardin: *The Game of Cards*
- 31   Richard Chew: *Lobster, Conanicut Island, Narragansett Bay*
- 35   Edgar Degas: *The Fallen Jockey*
- 37   Edgar Degas: *Edmondo and Therese Morbilli*
- 39   Edgar Degas: *Woman Ironing*
- 43   Robert Delaunay: *Political Drama*
- 45   Dianne Dickey: *Catfish*
- 47   Albrecht Durer: *St. Jerome and His Lion*
- 49   Domenico Ghirlandaio: *Lucrezia Tornabuoni*
- 51   Paul Gaugin: *Self-Portrait with Serpent*
- 53   Marsden Hartley: *Canuck Lumberman at the Beach*
- 55   Childe Hassam: *Allies Day, May 1917*
- 57   Childe Hassam: *The Wild Cherry*
- 59   Winslow Homer: *Sketch for Hound and Hunter*
- 61   Edward Hopper: *Nighthawks*
- 63   Jean-Auguste Dominique Ingres: *Ulysses*
- 65   Marie Laurencin: *Girl and a Dove*
- 67   Filippino Lippi: *Portrait of a Youth*

69 Edouard Manet: *King Charles Spaniel*
71 Edouard Manet: *La Gare St. Lazare*
73 Edouard Manet: *At the Races*
75 John Marin: *Woolworth Building No. 29*
77 Masolino da Panicale: *The Angel Gabriel*
79 Zivko Milic: *The Yellow Car*
83 Amadeo Modigliani: *Adrienne (Woman with Bangs)*
85 Claude Monet: *Bazille et Camille*
87 Claude Monet: *Lady with Parasol in the Garden*
89 Thomas Moran: *The Much Resounding Sea*
91 Berthe Morisot: *The Mother and Sister of the Artist*
93 Edvard Munch: *Gescgerei (The Scream)*
97 Kuzma S. Petrov-Vodhin: *The Bathing of the Red Horse*
99 Pablo Picasso: *Petrus Manach*
101 Pablo Picasso: *The Tragedy*
103 Camille Pissarro: *Hampton Court Green*
105 Camille Pissarro: *The Bather*
107 Camille Pissarro: *The Artist's Garden at Eragny*
109 Auguste Renoir: *Odalisque: Algerienne Reclining*
113 Megan Richard: *Moony Night*
115 Henri Rousseau: *Rendezvous in the Forest*
119 Georges Seurat: *Seascape, Port-de-Bessin, Normandy*
121 Suzanne Shelden: *The Heron*
123 Frans Snyders: *Still Life with Grapes*
125 George Stolt: *Clyde's Dock*
127 Gilbert Stuart: *Commodore Thomas Macdonough*
129 Henri de Toulouse Lautrec: *Another Night chez Le Moulin Rouge*
131 Henri de Toulouse Lautrec: *At the Café:*
133 Henri de Toulouse Lautrec: *Yvette Guilbert, diseuse/storyteller*
135 Ann Trentman: *No-Shows*
137 J.M. Turner: *Mortlake Terrace*
139 Remrandt van Ryun: *The White Cottage*
141 Domenico Veneziano: *Madonna and Child*

143 Edouard Vuillard: *Artist's Paint Box and Moss Roses*
145 Fantan-Latour, Degas, Toulouse-Lautrec, Gaugin, Van Gogh: *Self-Portraits*

149 Data on Artists and Paintings
150 Acknowledgments of Prior Publication of Poems
153 Biographical Note on Author

Preface

A Major Work
        By William Meredith

Poems are hard to read
Pictures are hard to see
Music is hard to hear
And people are hard to love

But whether from brute need
Or driving energy
At last, mind eye and ear
And the great sloth heart will move.

This will be the third collection of Elisavietta Ritchie's work we have been privileged to publish, and what a remarkable collection it is, rich imagination and a talent for metaphors the hallmarks of her work. Here we see a poet at the top of her game, and game is the precise word for the often whimsical accounts she gives of the painting on which she reflects. William Meredith's short poem seems an apt introduction to the book.

One thinks of Keats' critical touchstone, the concept of negative capability he proposes, the sensitivity and imaginative power an artist has to intuit even the very center of a cue ball, the ability of the individual to perceive, think, and operate outside the box. Poets often employ this symbiotic relationship with the visual arts, a literary device known as ekphraksis used to convey the deeper symbolism of the corporeal art form by means of a separate medium such as poetry. The poet contemplates a work of art and responds with a lifetime of experience and curiosity to imagine the world found in a given painting.

Here the poems are written in the voices of the artist, his wife (who might also be an artist), his mistress, his model, his dog—One thinks of the popular film in which all the characters in the paintings in a museum step from their frames and celebrate their liberation once the museum doors have closed for the night.

This seems a happy collaboration of artist and poet enhancing our understanding of a painting, as well as taking joy in the work from a verbal prospective. "How do I know what I think until I see what I say," I believe W.H. Auden once quipped.

In Chinese ideograms, a symbol for house combined with the figure of a stick woman within the house may be a symbol of peace. A plus B equals C, as it were, when a poet creates a new work standing on the shoulders of another artist creating something new under the sun.

An earlier title for this collection, *Glad I Gave My Art to All*, highlights what a long and distinguished career Lisa Ritchie has had. Perhaps only Grace Cavalieri is more prolific. When do these women sleep! I think of a William Meredith poem from *Hazard the Painter*, which tells the story of a 8-year-old Erica, a "factory of will," who when she returns from dancing class, "she dances!" Long may the dance continue for Lisa Ritchie and all her devoted followers who love how poetry can buoy the human spirit in the hands of such a fierce intelligence and curiosity.

–Richard Harteis

Author's Note

Except for several of these paintings given or shown to me by living artist friends, the paintings which inspired these poems are at the National Gallery, the Smithsonian, and available on the Internet. Many readers know the paintings or are content to imagine them.

The poems first trickled pour forth in December 1983, when writer Jonathan Agronsky gave me a 1984 engagement calendar with paintings from the National Gallery. The collection persisted in growing over the years. Page after page, painting after painting, for almost every painting a poem emerged.

Thanks to Jonathan Agronsky and those who helped with the final stages of *Reflections*: Richard Harteis, Barbara Shaw, the Calvert Library staff, and particularly Clyde H. Farnsworth for his long and invaluable support.

Reflections

Anonymous American: *Cat and Kittens*

That feline need
to commune

with a cat who needs
warmth as much as I do

but *these* cats beneath the parked
red pickup at the county dump—

> one fat white cat, black ears
> like bullet holes in his skull

> one black-and white Oreo
> hissing above her kittens,

> one twilight tabby tom
> who stakes out the trash—

these cats disdain a stranger
yet accept the passing violinist

she dumps milk and scraps
in paper bowls by the truck

otherwise people less
important than trees

trees yield shade squirrels birds
scratching posts and lofty refuge

humans only one step above
dogs who smell more terrible

John James Audubon: *Arctic Hare*

The Arctic hare can hop over the snow
and ice of the Bering Straits from Siberia,
escape unfriendly regimes unseen

through tunnels under the snow
over official borders on maps...
He travels at night. Up there

most of a winter day is night,
only a shine of vermillion
when on the horizon

skies slit apart for an hour
allowing creatures below
to recall the concept of light.

The sensible hare fears the teeth
of the fox, the Eskimo's snare, the artist
who kills his models to keep them still.

We too know how lonely and cold
our route unmarked in the snow,
how full of dangers our road.

John James Audubon: *Snowy Egret*

beside the canal

beached trains
gravel piles
rail yards
tangled tracks

tarps enshroud
peculiar shapes
cannot muffle cacophonies
screeches of steel

harsh whistles
horns and clanks
scritches of roaches
squeals of rats

a snowy egret
legs in slime
iridescent with oil
waits and croaks

John Woodhouse Audubon: *Long-Tailed Red Fox*
WHEN FOXES CAME CALLING

Does he know dusk his color, his hour, as for the mice, moles and voles who scurry through tunnels which lace our lawn in subterranean webs. I'd like to think he thinks altruistically (rule against anthropomorphism in literature?), is aware he does us a favor policing our scruffy garden.

He steps among tiger lilies, alert for whoever slips past underfoot, bottlebrush tail still as a stick. He eavesdrops, suddenly leaps, digs, bounds, pounces, nabs wind, lands with a look admitting he was outfoxed by a mouse, mole or vole...

II.
Our twin foxes also real, not images, similes or stand-ins for academic ideas. Juveniles, bibs white against rusty collars, they appear at our sliding glass garden door at four as if for a formal tea party, clotted cream, berry scones—

We serve stale kibbles our white angora shuns. Through the glass, she studies the visitors, who are aware I too am an observer. Neither Pusscat nor I twitch... Dish clean, the foxes turn, but pause, like ideas stashed away to examine later, expand upon, discard the next afternoon. I slide the door. Pusscat bounds down four crumbling brick steps, chases the invaders to the woods, satisfied, returns.

Next day they reappear at four...Their visits continue until the summer's end. Shots resound: hunting season open. Though they surely dove into dens up the winding dirt lane, but they never reappear in our garden.

III.
Still no foxes now! Rabbits returned since they disappeared four years ago so foxes should be sneaking back, flash of tail, eyes caught in headlights golden—

What is the parallel for which these could be metaphors? Notes unheard except inside the composer's skull waiting to grow to symphonies? Paintings visualized? An imagined plot but no pencil, pen or brush, only a stick on the sand?

My foxes are not metaphors but live critters now patrolling other woods unseen. But where? And where have they been?

Hendrick Avercamp: *A Scene on Ice*

few wear proper skates
or speed away
the instant they
hear the crack

only the hound
listens to life
under the ice
leaps to safer ground

our feet bare
we also dance
on thinning ice
hope to escape in time

Adolphe Blondheim: *The Decoration*

    THE WIDOW SPEAKS:

They give me a medal destined for *him*!
So I'm a widow who never was wife...
What use is this silver bauble?

Did my fleeting lover tell his captain
my girlhood name, where to find me?
Yes, I'm still here, ten long years...

Our dark-eyed boy will inherit this—
memento—from a father he never knew,
who never acknowledged him...

The boy holds an enormous glass jug:
this floated ashore from the ship
which bore his father away

to enlist in a stranger's war, fight
for a stranger's cause, for adventure,
and to escape his debts. Mine remain.

Our daughter picked oranges, filled a bowl,
we are hungry! But the artist insists he needs
the oranges for color, our faces so pale.

My dress is maroon, but he paints it dark
as my hair, as my life. What *lady* works
as a model? But I've kept on my clothes.

Has my darling abandoned other girls
in other lands? But he acknowledged *us,*
and *we* continue to grieve.

Mary Blumberg: *A Gift of Tomatoes*

You bring me the tight
       bloody suns of October
             snatched from vines
      entangled, which hide
emerald snakes and black-and-gold spiders.

Tomatoes escape from your basket of wicker,
       from your hands, through your fingers,
swell and explode inside
       my palms, bleed into my lines
of fate, highlight our destinies...

I try
   to tame them under my knife
       with salt and parsley and sugar

but their blood burns inside—
       their flesh ignites
           my throat like tinder—

I dream of gardens all winter
       where tomatoes loll, green, hard and icy,
           among shimmering snakes and furry spiders.

Then the carmine moon bursts through the sky—
                                    and I—

Pierre Bonnard: *Her Children*

Her children get into my paints!
They press palms sticky with jam
on my model! She wiggles, squeals!

My sister won't scold them.
They finger-paint on my canvas
their own destinies—

who'll become a burgher,
who a soldier, a priest,
my niece a courtesan!

Whatever métier
is fine with me
as long as it's not

another damned artist
who makes pictures all day,
babies all night.

Take your children out,
away, please, away!
I must work undisturbed!

Pierre Bonnard: *The Letter*

Admonition: don't waste my time
writing to a dying man—
He knows it, makes no bones—

I've written daily: my missives
might keep him alive. Maybe
they helped: he *had* to respond.

This is writing on tide soon to ebb,
on a pear which tomorrow will rot,
leaves which wither, crackle to freckles.

I scratch on wet cement. Illiterate
masons whose work must be paid
cover my words with bricks.

I try to carve love poems on rocks,
break my chisel's point.
One stone still needs my etch—

this will go on his grave.
Write now with smoke,
jet trails in a hurricane—

Still, I will write until
I too cannot form a word.

Mary Cassatt: *The Loge*

Shared lorgnettes view
the same play, same man.

Thank God *I'm* not twins.
Imagine two sets of eyes,
two secret scenarios.

At the entr'acte the man
must buy *three* champagnes.

He offers his coach,
returns us all home.

Outside their front door:
a confusion of tipsy kisses,
tangled disputes with each other.

Already they have forgotten
the plot of the play.

I have not. Nor have I
forgotten the man.

Paul Cezanne: *Still Life*

His oranges tinged with lime,
shadowed like evergreens,
are not perfect spheres.

The milk in his pitcher
curdles by the time
he puts down his brush,

peels oranges and eats.
Orange juice dribbles like varnish
over his sticky canvas.

        The potter on Telegraph Hill,
        my octogenarian neighbor,
        gave me her imperfect pots

        and one orange from her sill.
        Perfectly round. Then
        I ate three at once, admitted,

        "I feel green-round-the-gills,"
        "You are pregnant," she said.
        I grew imperfectly round.

        This dawn, I eat oranges
        round as the sun,
        it crowns through the sea,

        recall my imperfect peelings for
        an imperfect spouse, consequent
        crowning of an infant's head.

Each of our acts
sooner or later
affects another.

Paul Cezanne: *Man with Pipe*

No sweat, no threat: he puffed a *healthy* pipe.

The hollow shaft was weapon to repel intruders in his life
while he found the nail, scraped the bowl, dumped ash,
re-scraped, dumped, reamed, re-reamed, filled, tamped,
refilled, re-tamped, struck five Strike-Anywheres against
his soles, blew orbs of smoke, inhaled, blew more.

The whole procedure gave him time to organize defense.

Let guests sit and squirm, his mind deliberate not just
when age and drinking might excuse his long reflection.
We all thought him wise. He *knew* he was, his silence sage.

He was furious when I, trying to write, instead of macaroons
and fingernails to gnaw, unwrapped a pack of Chesterfields.
He'd never seen me light a match. I coughed and choked
as at age six, I gagged on pilfered Lucky Strikes.

A Scot, he was relieved: we'd save bucks if I did not
buy cigarettes. His Grade A pipe tobacco already cost a pile.

His cancer of the lungs was no surprise.
On this occasion he could not request his final guest,
Old Mister Death, to stand there while he cleaned his pipe.

Paul Cezanne: *Pyramid of Skulls*

They loved skulls, old masters, perched skulls
on linen cloths, boulders by a cave, piled
skulls in pyramids like friends with heads
close, deciphering by candlelight archaic texts.

A skull without a face or hat reveals the round
of bone, cranium almost-circular, no artifice.
The sinus hollows of the nose, sockets where
eyes used to be, emphasize absence, the stare.

If the artist tried to paint the eyes to follow
viewers through a gallery, forever haunt,
he gave up, figured best the viewer plunge
down wells, boney abysses, infinite depths.

Skull washed clean, the artist can repaint
the hapless fellow's history, re-invent life
and character. No one will correct him.
Sinners, paupers, monks, certain other

vocations, make skulls available to artists
who need models cheap. And not prone
to sneeze, chatter, criticize or eat. Nor will
the naked skull break pose to drink or pee.

Jean Simeon Chardin: *The Game of Cards*

That boy building a wall
of cards is cheating!

His cards are pleated so
they stand on the table's turf,

the king of hearts pokes
from the half-closed drawer.

What else in his pockets?
More hidden cards?

We all take a chance
with fragile constructions,

our gambles and gambols.
Yet what artist records

our efforts at architecture,
games in solitude?

Richard Chew: *Lobster, Conanicut Island, Narragansett Bay*

We sailed your twenty-foot Seabird,
crimson as passion is meant to be,
beached her between strata of slate,
built a driftwood fire, filled the pail.

While we waited for sea water to heat
you sketched the lobster...Combative!
Models are not meant to be.

Then you plunged him headfirst
into our now-boiling sea. I flinched—
You swore he died too fast to feel pain.

He turned scarlet: we dumped him onto
a slab of shale, cracked claws with stones,
pried the carapace with your marlin spike.

We tore him apart while you told me
Braque used fifty-nine different colors
(I'd labeled the paintings somber),
Picasso sketched on café tablecloths,
Cezanne never finished a work.

At eighteen you were already bound
for the Art Students League in New York.

Because we both dripped lobster juice
and sea and sky had turned dark,
we skinny-swam to the farthest buoy.

Out came the full moon,
flooded the ocean with light.

Boat again beached, you turned
your back. "Hurry," you urged.
"Get dressed before you catch cold!"

We shoved off, hoisted sail, reached port,
put the boat to bed, climbed the boatshed
to the moonlit roof, only talked.

Outside the cottage my mother rented,
your lips grazed my cheek. Your almost-kiss
entered a poem, first to see print. I was sixteen.

Autumn meant parting, departure.

For Christmas you sent me your favorite
'78s: *Tristan and Isolde*: "Love Duet"
and *Forza del Destino:* "Overture."

Best of all, your canvas fragrant with oil:
our lobster, green on the ocean floor.

We kept in only tenuous touch.

In a Soho gallery, decades later,
I discovered my portrait!
You must have sketched this
in your moonlight mind,
later painted in oils.
Too expensive to buy.

Where are you now? Still painting?
Are you even alive?

Your *Lobster* remains
bluegreen on my wall.

Edgar Degas: *The Fallen Jockey*

The jockey dressed in white jodhpurs
trots his stallion down the trail
for an equestrian competition.

He hopes to win silver cups to show off
when he climbs to the mountain hamlet, snatches
a maiden bride, rides with her into the night—

While he stops to pomade his hair, his horse
nibbles *Cannabis sativa,* heehaws and dances,
sashays off to eat buttercups...

The jockey holds a full glass of vodka.
He plans to jump like a Circassian, soar over
double rails without spilling a drop—

But he no longer dares hang from his saddle
to grab the kinjal stabbed in the ground,
or stand on the stallion's back,

or lead the charge of the heavy brigade
since his pot-head of a horse is sky-high,
shies at cannon, bugles and flags,

might well stumble and drop
vodka, maiden, jockey, and all
his noble intentions into the dust.

He nags his spaced-out horse to a stall,
pours oats laced with aspirin, downs
a full vessel of vodka, sprawls on the straw.

Wobbly jockey and lurching mount fall asleep.
The mountain's gene pools two-legged and four-
thus are never enriched with new sperm.

The maiden still pines on her distant peak...

Edgar Degas: *Edmondo and Therese Morbilli*

Her husband said, "*Ton portrait est si bon!*"
and hung the old canvas in their *salon*.

The carriage waits to drive her to Monoprix
for brushes and bras (hers now old as she),
but a call comes in from an avant-garde
painter who stopped by to leave her his card.

"I noticed your portrait—*Comme tu es belle!*
Our paths cross too late... I *totalement* fell—"

She writes back what both know, don't speak, don't dare:
"We would have had a cyclonic affair
so fertile for art...Life gave us no chance..."

She sighs, cries and savors their missed romance
en route to Monoprix clutching her list.

Paint brushes aren't cheap, like silk in her fist.
Brassieres are confusing, frightfully dear...
Ahhh! Black Lace Two-for-One! The choice is clear.

She unwraps one brand new black-lace brassiere,
dons spiderweb stockings—still owns a pair.
Her camisole is carmine (although the dye
derives from crushed beetles, female, who die)...

(See poem with Paul Gaugin's painting for continuation of this saga—)

Edgar Degas: *Woman Ironing*

Folding clothes,
I think of folding you
into my life.

Our king-sized sheets
like table cloths
for banquets of giants,

pillow cases, despite so many
washings, seams still
hold our dreams.

Towels orange and green,
flowered pink and lavender,
gaudy, bought on sale,

reserved, we said, for the beach,
refusing, even after years,
to bleach into respectability.

How many shirts and skirts and pants
recycling week after week, head
over heels recapitulating themselves!

All those wrinkles to iron…
Best ignore them…This year
wrinkles in style.

Myriad socks went paired into
the foam like creatures in the Ark.
Now single, they search for mates.

What's shrunk
is tough to discard
even for Goodwill.

In pockets, surprises:
forgotten matches,
lost screws clinking on enamel,

paper clips, whatever they held
between shiny jaws now dissolved
or clogging the drain;

well-washed dollars, legal tender
for all debts public and private,
intact despite agitation.

Look! Gleaming in the maelstrom:
one bright dime,
broken necklace of real gold

you brought from Kuwait,
the strangely tailored shirt
left by a former lover...

If you were to leave me,
if I were to fold
only my own clothes,

convexes and concaves of
blouses, panties, stockings, bras
turned upon themselves,

a mountain of unsorted wash
could not fill
the empty side of the bed.

Robert Delaunay: *Political Drama*

THE MAN AND THE WOMAN SPEAK

Spheres whirl and split!

Broken rainbows
can't connect their ends
Colors crash and run
green into lavender, blue against rose—

Dark silhouettes—

We struggle to push
through unhooked circles of gold
crimson and mauve
toward a target's core—

We are caught in the whirr of the wheel.

Even if the wheel slows
winds down to a stop
would we find ourselves
able to reach
the bull's-eye, the heart?

Dianne Dickey: *Catfish*

The children haul the oyster cage
dripping seaweed to the dock
with two whiskered giants—

Dream fish of cat-fishermen.
They nail the head to a board.
One flick of their filet knife

slits the uncertain chin.
They peel skin away like
a condom or sock.

With a flowered towel, I seize
one huge head, avoid spines,
rows of teeth...

We've neither hammer nor nails.
My tiny penknife, silver, nicks.
The catfish tries to wrest free.

I slash one belly, need
pliers, cleavers, marlin spikes,
first aid—

Aghast at entrails,
                you
                        just stand...

I'm told you are hung like
an elephant: does *castration*
flash through your mind?

The children watch life
rebelling finally quiet, fetch a pail
to rinse the filets clean.

You like my catfish stew
and make a proposition.
I turn you down.

Albrecht Durer: *St. Jerome and His Lion*

Like St. Jerome, we need to keep
lions dozing by our beds, their paws
across our blankets while we sleep.
Affectionate despite the claws,

in winter lions are comforters
(we lack the monk's thick warming cowls).
They lull us with their regal purrs,
guard with deep locomotive growls.

Lions smaller when the times were saintly,
the artists' eyes had seldom seen
real lions in savannahs, daintily
eating antelope, bloody, lean.

True, table manners aren't well-bred.
Housebreaking them becomes a chore.
But why stare at a human head?
You won't find your live lion a bore.

We meditate upon a skull,
already know what's in our own.
We quickly learn what *lions* mull:
they lick their lips, our cheeks: *fine bones.*

Domenico Ghirlandaio: *Lucrezia Tornabuoni*

LUCREZIA SPEAKS

A sad fate I foresaw
for my firstborn son, as if I knew
he would not live to manhood.

Could I have foretold the shriek
as the wooden piano seat
spun its final arpeggios?

Paul Gaugin: *Self Portrait with Serpent*
THERESE MORBILLI SPEAKS

...Now! *Café au lait* with my artist love,
that one with fake halo floating above.
He's just returned from some duty-free isle
where weather's too hot and bras not in style.

He shares his oil paint and turpentine smell—
I always fear everybody can tell...

My lover's herpetological bent
unnerves me, but now my beauty is spent
I'm relieved his eyesight has gone askew...

Black lace will hide years! Hèlas, quite a few...

Before either crosses that River Styx
we set out for one more quick caffeine fix—

Marsden Hartley: *Canuck Yankee Lumberjack, Old Orchard Beach, Maine*

The summer artists stand apart,
adjust their easels, mix their paints,
size up, hasten to capture

sowers and reapers,
millworkers, stonecutters,
fishermen, sailors,

ship builders,
spinners at wheels,
tenants on abandoned farms,

all foreign to their own
winter studios
and social circles.

But oh, for the lobster
and that swarthy bather
whatever their provenance

I want *now, alive*—

Childe Hassam: *Allies Day, May 1917*
THE VETERANS SPEAK

So many flags!
Give us this day
our daily flags.

Let us wave flags at others
as they would wave at us
a thousand hands,
ghost hands thrust up
from our far-flung graves...

Patriotic clichés
spin silver cobwebs
up the poles to our skulls.

Wrap me in the stars,
the stripes on our backs—

So many crosses...

Childe Hassam: *The Wild Cherry*
    Mesimarja *Rubus arcticus*

We drink liqueur bled from red berries
which grow near the Arctic pole
beneath a white sun

tumble down obsidian slopes
of volcanoes unmentioned on maps

somersault into people wearing iron bits
load their mules with sacks of obsidian
while they trudge uphill and down

we slide past
encounter jungles of briars
alive with cobras
we try to appease them with toads

hands emptied
heads bare we escape,
roll down to grassy hills
pause dizzy in lilies and mint
love
whirl away
bounce on moss

everyone's spinning
skies reel

we splash into a pond
transform into trout
change to swans admiring our rippled reflections

now wingtip to wingtip
we soar ever higher beneath a black sun

Winslow Homer: *Sketch for Hound and Hunter*
THE HUNTER SPEAKS

We will all drown

I grab
the horns of the stag
who may drag us to shore

unless he can guess
I fired the shot
that tumbled him
bleeding into the stream

He cannot know

Of course he knows
we need his fur, his hide,
his flesh

Whatever he senses
the river is deep,
the night freezing dark

and we
are terribly far from home.

Edward Hopper: *Nighthawks*
A CUSTOMER SPEAKS

At midnight I enter the diner.

The lady there has copper hair,
scarlet dress, décolleté.

Beside her, the man wears
a dark suit, dark tie, blue shirt.
He keeps his fedora on indoors.
Does he lack manners?
Or else he expects a quick exit.

Yet his cigarette
was just lighted, white
coffee mug untouched.

His nose is sharp as the dent
in his hat for whatever news
soda jerk or the lady convey.

Her left arm rests on the counter,
fingers so close they could touch
his right hand. They do not.

Alone at the opposite counter
I too wear my hat indoors,
rearrange the condiment bottles.

The soda jerk, tense, divines I can't pay.
Yet one cup free, he may reckon,
is worth his life, or mine.

I stir in all the sugar and cream,
pat the gun in my jacket
head out for the bus.

Jean-Auguste Dominique Ingres: *Ulysses*

ULYSSES SPEAKS

Rats in my beard
Lice in my hair

Sun and storm chap
the hook of my nose

Around my eyes
salt writes a warning

My coolie hat
melts in the rain

Crazy to wear red but
this is my one shirt

saved for homecoming
I'm impatient but

Everywhere birds
are waiting to land

I wait to land
without going aground

but birds and I
are still at sea

Marie Laurencin: *Girl and a Dove*

Notes of silk float over meadows dull
with August drought... *April's mating trills*!

Forget it, bird, no would-be mate
returns unseasonal calls so late.

Fly home, repair your messy nest
not woven with a wren's finesse

but stuck one twig upon the next,
lost game of pick-up-sticks, a mess

prey to hurricanes. No point to rebuild.
Low market for wrecked real estate...Unwilled,

the dust of August dimmed last spring's
hatpin eyes, glistening head and wings.

You'll never soar like gull and hawk
or dive to nab some mole you stalk

or plummet osprey-style for fish or bait.
You're stuck with seeds, so face your fate:

Love-calls now indecent...Your bill-
and-coos *are* haunting these fields still

and your departure agitates
the air...Sudden echoes, desperate—

You reappear, re-paired
by a new troubadour!

So, on with coos, and on with love! Although
you must remember how these matters go...

Filippino Lippi: *Portrait of a Youth*

Those hazel eyes!
O, oh...oh...

Edouard Manet: *King Charles Spaniel*
THE SPANIEL SPEAKS

I am King Charles' well-bred dog.
Daily the king's valet brushes
my long auburn ears, white coat.

When I yip
I get bits
from the king's gold plate.

From the king's parapets
I look down on the mutt
who patrols the lake.

I *am* superior...Still,
I would like to slum it
beyond castle walls,

probe shady alleys
with intriguing scents
and careless garbage pails

where that mongrel
wolfs his trophies down
with canine relish

and humps the ill-bred
bitch in heat...
I yearn for such fun!

Edouard Manet: *La Gare Saint-Lazare*

    THE LADY SPEAKS

I wait for the train
with the black locomotive
which wears a bouquet
of phlox in the window.

I am tired of waiting
every day at the station,
so is your daughter,
so is your dog!

If you don't arrive
by tonight, I'll buy tickets
to Cannes for the winter
with other lovers.

If at last you arrive from Marseilles,
you will find my flat bare
but for one blue satin bow
and a strand of dark auburn hair.

Yet if you arrived with bouquets
of tulips, and your usual excuses,
I'd prepare *rognons de veau*
and bake a *torte aux cerises*.

I've forgiven others who came
hungry and tired and late.
One turned up with daisies
at four a.m. That one, I wed.

But oh, this terrible smoke
and noise of the trains!
How long must we wait?
How long this time will you stay?

Edouard Manet: *At the Races*

A stableful waits at the gate, impatient for ribbons, cups,
scrubbed and curried—coats gleam and manes shine.
Bets on a winner remain to be placed at the track.

Fine breeding, manners forgotten, they crowd, nip and kick.
The ungainly lot demands water, exercise, oats. One shies at
the gate, another smashes barricades, a third refuses to jump.

The filly named Cinderella keeps losing her shoes. A jockey
falls in the pond, while his mount gallops to finish first—
The judge disqualifies him: lack of a rider to guide his reins.

A light-footed gelding smells clover, gorges until he bloats.
Six colts escape from the lot, chew jimsonweed, get high,
roll in mud, dance like circus ponies on a Woodstock week.

Cinderella, horseshoes renailed, breaks from the pack, sprints—
loudspeaker bellows *First.* Spectators weep: no one had bet on
the frivolous filly. Her owner sheds joyful tears, counts his cash.

The stallion Zeus, his jockey in harlequin colors, wins Second,
chases the filly and mounts her amid guffaws from the crowd.
Neglected horses graze turf until dusk, fall asleep on the hoof.

Yet a few limp forth, bellicose neighs prove *they're* still on track.
Dear stories, my thoroughbreds, you slip from my desk, trot to
the yard, break into a canter, jump the fence into the world—

A new race every week.

John Marin: *Woolworth Building No. 29*
THE WINDOW WASHER CONSIDERS THE SCENE

Such clutter in here to examine but
from the seventieth floor I get vertigo
looking *out* through oversized panes.
Too high for even a Mohawk
not supposed to fear heights.

I crane my eyes up, catch snatches
of blue, ripped clouds, snowflakes, ash.
Too many lights to see stars.

In rain the flat becomes an aquarium,
in blizzards an igloo aloft. Any season,
river below brims with flotsam, jetsam:

storms and people toss artifacts, fishermen
cast while their baskets and fish guts escape,
plastic and Styrofoam, good stuff and bad,
and kayaks, canoes, sculls and toy boats,
pine and magnolia cones, petals, bouquets,
corsages, lost logs, riverine critters, dogs,
cats who could not swim well as urban alligators.

Always unmentionable trash.

Unseen underwater: odd bodies, feet
in concrete, nourish the bottom-feeders.

Reflected wherever: my face.

Yet if I am quick, for an instant I might
snag the vagrant moon sliding past—

Masolino da Panicale: *The Angel Gabriel*

God is a quick-change artist, many-handed.
He surprises the angels as well
as those of us suspended
partway between heaven and hell.

Each day a blizzard, flood or drought,
somewhere plague, war or volcanoes explode.
It's the lone suicide whom we care about,
the avalanche which wipes out our own road.

Zivko Milic: *The Yellow Car*

A foreign writer and dangerous friend
(did he smuggle out swiped documents? I had
none to steal) as relief from his journalist job

painted the rainy Mass Ave and 13th St scene
below his Spartan walk-up front window
onto a long cardboard box found in a bin.

Focal point: one yellow car (maybe a cab)
solitary behind a skinny winter-stripped oak.
Did this tree stand for his native land?

His first try with a Swiss Artist Kit, rare behind
the Iron Curtain. *Here,* both rooms came alive
with perfectly-painted art forbidden there—

dissident nudes in sinuous greens and blues, six
starving bodies twisted gray from a gulag, a lone
farm: one cow, one hut, two lovers, full moon.

He painted on plywood, on planks, trash-can lids,
cartons, boards, whatever we swiped at night
from abandoned construction sites.

My traveling husband of safer sorts
thought him quite safely gay.
My friend was not,

and taught me to take risks
with words, life, and love,
lessons I practice still.

A black airport shuttle drove him away
for his farewell flight. He was broke. I paid
the fare, $200. His art remains on my walls.

No one likes his work except
fellow artists who recognize skill
and I who harbor them all.

One canvas, black on white, *Thinking Girl*,
wears my face. Let this be the cover of my
final book. I will credit him.

                         ***

After 25 years, we meet again in his now
less dangerous land. He discarded his art.
We both remain writers, and yes,

he remembers *The Yellow Car*
and the swiped afternoons
we did not spy on the view.

Amadeo Modigliani: *Adrienne*
THE WOMAN WITH BANGS SPEAKS

I study the artist who
celebrates my extended neck,
slit onyx eyes,
and cassis-red lips.

My nose is a ski jump,
hands pale orange lumps!
My sideburns are too dark
and should be clipped.

Do we both get away with murder?
He calls my almond eyes
the eyes of an icon, or lion.
They do know how to look.

He steals out my door…
I spy through the panes
as he fills in his sketch
au Café des Espoirs Perdus.

He dips his pen unaware
in his cassis, sweetens the lips
as he sweetened mine
with dark-cherry kisses and wine.

Claude Monet: *Bazille et Camille*

The grass is green,
her dress is white
as the late snow
he throws in her path.

He wants to love
her white body...

He loosens his white
cravat because
his weather is warm,
asks if she needs
his spectacles to see
the symbol of his intentions.

He makes a proposition—

She turns him down:

"Any man who keeps on
his hat while courting
is out of the running...

And you *should*
wash your beard."

Claude Monet: *Lady with a Parasol in a Garden*
    THE LADY SPEAKS

I slip through flowering crowds,
avoid bees schooling around.
A parasol shades my face from the sun,
from bee-stingers, trickster eyes.

My petticoats skim peony beds,
other beds where I've slept
or not slept or still might—
who is to know?

I glide through this garden
as through a novel-in-progress...
Observer-scribe, I imagine,
perceive, take notes—

Like that spider, long-legged, Latin name* longer,
I hang out near azaleas, inspect a neglected web,
weigh which fly, gnat or smaller arachnid to nab,
mandibles to crunch, then devour at dusk...

                                              Pholous phalangiodes

Thomas Moran: *The Much Resounding Sea*

THE SKIPPER SPEAKS

The sea resounds too much
has no compunctions
or discriminations

but thrashes and whirls
my anxious ark

flings water in her bilge
would break her wormy ribs
suck splinters down the maelstrom

Waves toss flotsam like shuttlecocks
into the foam and
sailors like wisps of straw

As opposed to my love
for the ocean

my logical fears
of mortality
and decapitation
impress me more

Both will come

I won't die right off
though this might
be preferable

Faced with brevity of span
when I should cherish
every second I waste
too many days afloat
on oceans of intentions

Even the beach
is no longer safe

Berthe Morisot: *The Mother and Sister of the Artist*
    THE LADIES SPEAK

In the parlor we read
papers and books, speculate

is the unknown prisoner
one of ours? Is he dead?

I already wear black.
If in white, I'd not feel involved—

Still caught in my dream of last night's
Grand Bal and live duke at the palace—

Edvard Munch: *Gescgerei (The Scream)*

Small boats involved with lines and seines
in the far fjord, and distracted passersby
on the long pier, uninterested in why,
ignore the scream.

My scream now, silent outside
the city jail Visitation Room.

I forgot my photo ID, can't pass the gate.
No documents, I'm unknowable,
potentially dangerous to jailors, jailbirds.
So blown, my chance to talk on closed-circuit
TV with a manic son gone off his meds.

Changed from gentle collie to rabid coyote,
he picked a fight, fell asleep by the curb.
Cops picked him up, locked him up.

In court, chains wind around his gray
jail bodysuit unwashed a week.

Out here, this wooden bench
painted glossy gray is sticky
and hard on bones.
Inside the Visitation Room, armchairs
marked SHERIFF have cushioned seats.
The sheriff's revolver is real. My son
had none. Prison barber buzz-cut both.

A lady with blond wool hair, flowered
camisole over gleaming chocolate skin,
comes outside to sympathize.

"Good to sit here," she says. "Cold inside."
Her older son is a Correction Officer.
Her younger son's locked up.

"But he be home in June, bless the Lord."
She talked with him, (the Lord, the son,
on remote TV). Her thirty minutes talking
time not all used up, his kids take a turn.

"He'll need you to deposit cash," she says,
"for thermals and a snack. You feed bills
in that red box—takes only twenties and
the guards skim three bucks off first."

What do I know of the system, the law,
heights and depths of another's pain,
only know we both must try
to set things right.

All the while, beyond *these* walls
in near coves, small boats involved
in lines and seines also sail
in circles of ripples,

and distracted passersby down pier
and bench pay no heed to the scream.

Kuzma S. Petrov-Vodhin: *The Bathing of the Red Horse*

bare butt on bare back
by the river edge

the naked rider
on a bare chestnut mare

wants them both
to swim across

but the mare is wary
of swirling waves

and you know what they say
about horses and water

she whinnies and rears
and the naked rider

slides into the drink
quick as her wink—

Pablo Picasso: *Petrus Manach*
THE WIFE SPEAKS

Can't You Tell I'm Working?

I can't say that. He wants to talk.
He could have seen my fingers tap.
He *needs* to chat so I can't hide, or flip.

Must smile, inquire, "You'd like some tea?"
Up to me to tweak the stove. "Must buy more coal,
the water's cold, takes time to heat..."

"Good time for conversation then,
time to eat another meal."
He's pleased with his creative time today.

I've not half used up mine—sixteen personae
on the loose, in limbo caught, their destinies
unsolved—if I pause they'll slip away—

"Did you pay these bills?"   "Not due this week."
"Where are my pills?"   "There, in your paints."
"And what's for lunch?"   "No time, no francs..."

I clean my spectacles with vigor, crack
one lens. My parched notebooks thirst
for words, my brain leaks paragraphs.

Outsiders think me cheerful, kind. I don't shirk
scrubbing his paint-splattered shirts,
burnt-out cooking pots. I darn his socks.

So I can't be unseemly, scream,
Leave me alone, my love,
for God's sake, let me also work!

Pablo Picasso: *The Tragedy*

is knowing this
the beach between

sea with no boat
shore with no home

the lost cannot
be remade

night is chill,
feet bare, clothes thin

child's fingers too small
to seize what might be

behind the bluff
dogs strain on their chains

Camille Pissarro: *Hampton Court Green*
THE PRISONERS SPEAK

We march across
spring-fragrant green.

The unseen sun
dapples Astroturf.

Red brick buildings
could be Harvard Yard,

they waits for us to investigate
beyond our microcosm—

The sky, washed out,
clouds impressionistic.

Only walls are real.
We can't *live* here—

We can't escape.
In single file

we march for years
while sun turns rooftops gold.

Camille Pissarro: *The Bather*

THE MODEL SPEAKS

I must have been beautiful back then,
am still surprised how many men pursued...

I let them think me but a starchy prude
until we paddled up the river when
the day was fair, light yellow, blue and green.

I was afraid the sun would leave
freckles on my breasts and we'd conceive
an unexpected child from where we'd been
cavorting in the shallows by the bank
of tiger lilies, peppermint and moss—

We yearned for more, but foliage was dank
with spilled champagne and sticky with cassis.

A need to pee, then nettle stings, kept me
from further loss of maidenhood ...
Each loss is the first, and never quite the same.
Those early days, I never understood.

I have made many famous but forget their names,
dear artists who would sketch me in the nude...

I was a willing model: French plumbing then was crude
so they would scrub me till I shone, then came
to hang on these renown museum walls,
my loveliness immortalized in paint.

Although my grandmothers would faint,
I have no regrets I gave to art my all.

Camille Pissarro: *The Artist's Garden at Eragny*
HIS WIFE SPEAKS

How can I get back to sleep
this warm April dawn?

He woke me up to complain
he cannot sleep at all.

In fact, he was snorting and snuffling
all night like a boar after truffles

while I was dreaming in colors
all the flowers we would buy.

Awake, I recall: *no francs for plants
till he sells a painting.* His oils are all wet.

I steal into the night. Full moon
shows patches his dog dug bare

while *he* was stretching his costly *toiles*
and daubing paint on his models.

My apron pockets hide seeds,
bulbs sprout in my drawers.

I plant larkspur, peonies, hollyhocks,
zinnias, marigolds for their ruffled suns.

At eight he awakes. "*Regardes, ma cherie*!
While we slept, blossoms leapt from my palette!

But where is my *café au lait*?
And we cannot eat posies for supper."

To survive through next winter
I plant rutabagas, potatoes and leeks,

scrub mud from my fingers,
sprinkle nightshade on his vichyssoise.

Auguste Renoir: *Odalisque: Algerienne Reclining*
THE GYPSY SUMMONED BEFORE THE COMMANDANT

Your questions I don't understand
but in the word "interrogation" I hear
terror...I know no names.

In the past, those who questioned me
wanted facts, histories, and names.
I know nothing about anyone till he asks.

Then I see through skin and skull,
trace seines of lines and lives...and lies.
I never forget a hand...I know no names.

I hold the sperm of half of Europe in my womb.
My Gypsy babies steal across the earth.
I know no names.

I have deciphered death in every palm.
I fear the gleam of your instruments.
I know no names.

Look, I am old. My skirts are dank
from your jail. My silver tarnished,
you stole my gold.

Yet my hair remains dark, my leg slim,
I still shake a fine tambourine—
could show you a good time.

Come, dismiss those surly guards at the gates.
Tear up your reports. Beyond these walls
my caravan awaits us both.

I could reveal the future of your regime.
I'd read your own fortune free.
Come along...I can tell you now:

The lines on my palm
are longer than yours.
And I know your name.

Megan Richard: *Moony Night*

I extol full moon nights
how even if storms
bandage the sky
my energy roars,
new work billows forth.

"*We* dread full moons,"
says the RN over our tea.
"That's when the loonies
tend to hit the ER."
She studies me sideways.

I slap down a ten
for unfinished pastries,
wish her good night shifts,
run home through twilight
crazed with flames.

In time I'll go blind
so while the lunatic moon
crowns from the sea
must write fast
snatch at stars—

Henri Rousseau: *Rendezvous in the Forest*

The captain and a lady not his
are kissing deep in the wood
for eternity caught in the act.
Both sit on one horse, dappled gray,
patient with squirms on his back.

I met my Paris-born émigré
and would-be *amour*
au Foret de St. Cloud
as the sun split the sky.

Our rusty bicycles parked by a pine,
we curled upon spongy moss.
I must depart the next day.

Though he stood at the top
of his Grande Ecole physics class,
his professor informed him
"*Vous n'etes pas vraiment français.*
No *bourses* for immigrants."

Must love in Paris always be lost?

Had we one horse instead
of two broken bikes, we might
have ridden from the forest together.

I sailed away. He stayed,
worked in a research lab.
Each found a logical spouse.

Years later I landed briefly in Paris.
We met while I nursed a child
in a one-star hotel near
le Jardin de Luxumbourg
where we used to meet every day.

His doctor had just informed him
his wife's stillborn infant
could not have been his: *X-rays
long had rendered him sterile.*

Later she mailed me a card
edged in black with a note:
"radiation overexposure."

I know he mostly died
of a broken heart
as happens in Paris.

        Hoof prints of that dappled horse
        remain on the forest floor,
        mottled tracks
        of four bicycle tires
        still indent the green mud.

Georges Seurat: *Seascape at Port-de-Bessin, Normandy*

bluffs where Nazis built
pillboxes and cannon,
beaches where they scattered
giant jacks to thwart D-Day,
the Allies' LSTs, soldiers, tanks.

Waves caught those
who failed to reach
safety on land.

In kinder times
generations of artists
paint in splashes and dots
these yellow-green hills,
bluffs, sands and sea,

and ladies in dresses
ankles to chin,
decades later
in and out of bikinis.

still sun and bathe
and sail in the waves,

as if nothing had happened here.

Suzanne Shelden: *The Heron*

Aide-Memoire for Czeslaw Milosz, poet in exile

The great blue heron skims
soy bean fields
stripped by the harvester.

The lance of his neck probes wind.
Wide wings flap with languor
as if slowed by December.

He rises above bare hawthorns,
blackberry canes enclosing the pond
like barbed wire. You recall

storks on village roofs of childhood,
your solitude and flights...Your losses flood
over you like tide in the marsh.

The heron soars over battalions
of cattails and Johnson grass, to the river,
disappears beyond channel markers,

but flings his shadow on furrows
where dried stalks bristle and
leftover velvet pods still hold seed.

Frans Snyders: *Still Life with Grapes*

I washed grapes by hand
in a tub of galvanized iron
while a young man

whose name I cannot recall
directed a green garden hose
at the fruit and at me.

Hot day when Monsieur Snyders
painted my portrait, did the young man
aim the hose to cool me? Or so

I'd remove and wring out my dress?
Something sexual in his intentions?
I was sixteen, I think.

I study the painting now, recall
My curls slipped from a crimson scarf,
the young man's curls as damp as mine...

I inhale the fragrance of grapes,
taste wine from a previous vintage,
recall the delights of sluicing fruit,

how I stripped grapes into the vat,
nibbled those darkest and sweetest,
till gold-and-black hornets swarmed.

Oh! how those hornets stung!
But oh, how he soothed my skin
with kisses of newly-pressed wine...

George Stolt: *Clyde's Dock*

Not a dock to warrant portraiture
although you painted piles
mahogany streaked with gold.

No fancy wharf with winches, lifts or slips,
parasol or picnic bench. Our ladder barnacled
and mossed, steps were broken, gone.

The hurricane ripped off and stole our boards—
a stranger's planks came floating back,
Someone's staircase landed in our marsh
as if to let us climb the sky.

We must plane smooth some stranger's boards,
pound flat the popped-up nails, re-varnish all...

Sunken tugs and fishing boats impede navigation.
Low tide the cove is sand and mud and ice,
lost rudders and abandoned anchors.
Cove too shallow anyway for deeper keels.

Crab pots survive, hold hapless perch.
Crabs wait to pinch a toe, a rod, a line
with dangled chicken backs.

Gulls paint the lower dock a Jackson Pollack free.
Swallows nest beneath, soar at eventide.
Wasps also lurk beneath the joists, poise to sting—

You knew someday you'd need a pier,
a friendly port to sail or paddle toward or swim
before the fiercer hurricane took you—

And now it has, will take us all...

National Gallery of Art, Washington, D.C.; Andrew W. Mellon Collection (1942.8.17)

Gilbert Stuart: *Commodore Thomas Macdonough*

Delicious when the ghost
of someone you never managed to sleep with
on waking days

one night returns in dress uniform
your feather quilt is shaken out, puffed up,
you are fragrant with lavender soap.

How do you greet revenants?
This time, how could you resist him?
Yet this time, how could you?

This happens in dreams and seems safe,
but beware: one revenant
could take you away with him.

Henri de Toulouse Lautrec: *Another Night chez Le Moulin Rouge*

Those fancy ladies in a queue
are going *where*

their nether parts
so shockingly unclothed?

Bulges, bruises, bumps
show on buttocks, thighs.

The auburn-haired lady hikes
her skirts and hides her face,

another shows
half a smile.

Amused? Embarrassed? Smug?
Made a mint last night?

But they know
where they're going.

Henri de Toulouse Lautrec: *At the Café:*
THE ANEMIC CASHIER SPEAKS

Not one of my suitors interests me
for a long-term alliance...Those
who *are* interesting don't suit—

too old or too young, too fat or too thin,
one lacks a job, another loves work too much,
all relish the absinthe I pour.

Those who intrigue me already have
wives with more money than I
and their feline claws leave scars.

I love men who beguile me
with wondrous stories, chocolates, champagne,
while they spin on and on, then would love me all night

but *I* need to sleep! Must unlock the café at dawn,
mop the floors clean, count yesterday's cash, await
my next dalliance, splash on more perfume.

Henri de Toulouse Lautrec: *Yvette Guilbert, diseuse/storyteller*
THE LADY GIVES ADVICE

When your lover invites you to join him
at dinner with his old flame
who just blew into town,

wear your barest black dress,
black fishnet stockings,
sandals with gold spiked heels.

Choose the jewellery which
is unmistakably real,
preferably his most recent gift.

Curl your hair, kohl your eyes.
You're not as young as you used to be.
Hope she is even older.

Restock you purse with lipstick,
an avant-garde shade of rouge,
expensive perfume,

and mad money enough
to send you all home in separate cabs.
Should you be first to arrive

at the medium-priced café he chose
or give them a chance to talk?
This once you will not be late.

Forget you are fighting
a fever. Perhaps
she will catch it too.

File your nails to a point,
button your long black gloves
and sally into the dark.

Ann Trentman: *No-Shows*

I wanted all of you live!

Why did some die
en route to the party?
The best even fell
before leaving home.

Others, long dead, creep
through garden windows,
the kitchen door, half drunk
bottles in hand, years late.

What can I offer now—
flat beer, vinegar-wine,
anemic champagne?

Cockatoos finished the caviar,
roaches the camembert,
mice left trails on the plates.

True, we've all changed.
New lines etch our palms.

Will we have voices to sing?
Hands to applaud?

Yet we agreed to greet
New Year's together again.
The table is set.
My blackberry vodka is chilled.

I expect you at ten.

J.M. Turner: *Mortlake Terrace*

The artist could not resist
painting Artist at Easel
painting View of the Lake.

Maupassant described *l'artiste*
at the edge of the circle
watching himself
smack in the center while
also standing outside the circle
watching himself watch himself

Here the artist is painting
The Artist Painting Himself, the lake
and the dog patrolling the shoreline

The dog may be watching his own
unstable reflections in the lake

The artist sits in the shade
too far from the edge
to observe his reflection

Or does he reflect at all
in or on the lake
on himself or his work

The lake is fixed
His subjects forever are
caught one hundred percent
in the moment

Rembrandt van Ryun: *The White Cottage*

The windmill waits
for the miller, the wind,
for flood tide to pass,
bulbs round its base to sprout.

Sky breaks with light
over the flat dark land,
the best the sun
can do today.

But today the miller
went to the village
to sell his flour
and visit his barber.

We will wait for the miller,
for tulips to bloom,
for seas to subside
before the dikes split

and snatch the instant
flowers or muffled sun
or barbered miller appear
to escape the flood and the frame—

Domenico Veneziano: *Madonna and Child*

That sweet baby's gonna
give his innocent mama
a tentful of trouble.

The glint in his eyes,
twist of his lips,
predict *mischief maker*

He will tip over tables,
stay too late with his elders,
hang out with riffraff.

Not stubby hands of an artist
who messes with charcoal and paint
or patterns rocks in the yard—
The Mother's long smooth fingers
show a lover of culture
and spiritual matters.

She will waste time
dreaming notable futures
for the whole family.

Not the typical carpenter's wife.
What peculiar guests
she entertains: those wings!

She may not find time
to sweep up Joe's sawdust,
or properly diaper the Infant.
Let's observe how
she raises that Child!

As for those halos of gold—
Both have auburn hair.
You know what they say
about redheads—watch out!

Edouard Vuillard: *Artist's Paint Box and Moss Roses*
THE ARTIST SPEAKS

My pitcher holds milk,
lemonade or blood,
this time embraces pink-to-plum roses.

I brought home the bouquet
to atone for painting all day—
my models take such splendid poses—

drinking all night in the café,
then helping home through the mud
that magnificent flower-seller—

So now as pink tendrils flood the sky
and dawn breaks like an ostrich egg
I bring to my wife this peace bouquet—

Degas, Self Portrait

Fantin-Latour, Toulouse Lautrec, Degas, Van Gogh:
SELF PORTRAITS

1.
The artists' faces wear
farouche expressions

van Gogh one
half-green brow

unwashed peach-pit skin
red hair /red beard

Degas' surprise oriental cast
where did his parents hang out

Did the artists chew brushes
as I chew my pencil

peer into eyes which shine
from the glisten of oil

like animal eyes
mine in the night

yet they permit me
portholes into their souls

how *my* eyes hurt
I go blind inside galleries

Won't all these colors inform
my soul so the rest of my life

inside my eyes I will see
the revenge of the artists

women in colorful wedges
dappled reflections of bridges

boats and banks of the Seine
laundresses washing/ironing/sorting

naked bathers cavorting
(mosquitoes/nettles/snakes hide in underbrush)

2.
In the gallery café the tourists
in patterns, pastels and plaids

check cell phones
gray government types

in gray suits   white shirts
striped red-and-blue ties

furtively check Blackberries
and gobble lunch

My pointillist salad gleams
with russet raisins, black beans

sunflower seeds
lettuce and spinach leaves

ellipses and dots
red curves of red peppers

recalcitrant stems of broccoli florets
fight my Swiss Army knife

create a Georges Seurat
scattered by Jackson Pollack

The artists fought their Parisian critics
who hurled palette knives at the avant-garde

3.
A black-bearded young man
plaid shirt forest green

wears a gray fedora indoors
this broiling day

chews on his pencil
as I my pen

could he be sketching me
as I pick at slippery salad

more likely his own Self-Portrait
My eyes would explore

his split soul   How solipsistic
interdependent we artists are

Is he merely a German accountant
calculating expenses

I *must* return to the gallery
Thunderstorm breaks   water cascades

In haste I leave my tray
on the turning turntable

circle behind him
If he was indeed sketching me

while I was writing
should I ask

He turns the lined
3 X 4 notebook

I glimpse the page
the paper is blank

Notes on the Artists

John James Audubon: 1785-1851
John Woodhouse Audubon: 1812-1862
Adolphe Blondheim: 1888-1969
Mary Blumberg: Living artist
Pierre Bonnard: 1867-1947
Mary Cassatt: 1844-1926
Paul Cezanne: 1839–1906
Jean Simeon Chardin: 1699-1779
Richard Chew: 1929-
Edgar Degas: 1834–1917
Dianne Dickey: 1945-
Edouard Vuillard: 1868–1940
Ignace-Henri-Jean-Theodore Fantan-Latour: 1836-1904
Paul Gaugin: 1848-1903
Domenico Ghirlandaio: 1449-1494
Marsden Hartley: 1877-1943
Childe Hassam: 1859 –1935
Winslow Homer: 1836-1910
Edward Hopper: 1882–1967
Jean-Auguste Dominique Ingres: 1780–1867
Filippino Lippi: 1459–1504
Edouard Manet: 1832–1883
John Marin: 1870–1953
Zivko Milic: 1923-2011
Amadeo Modigliani: 1884–1920
Claude Monet: 1840–1926
Thomas Moran: 1837–1926
Berthe Morisot: 1841-1895
Edvard Munch: 1863–1944
Masolino da Panicale: c. 1383– c. 1447
Kuzma S. Petrov-Vodhin: 1878-1939
Pablo Picasso: 1881–1973
Camille Pissarro: 1830–1903
Auguste Renoir: 1841–1919
Megan Richard: Living artist
Henri Rousseau: 1844–1910
Georges Seurat: 1859–1891

Suzanne Shelden: Living artist
Frans Snyders: 1579-1657
George Stolt: 1958-2015
Gilbert Stuart: 1755–1828
Henri de Toulouse Lautrec: 1864–1901
Ann Trentman: 1950-
Joseph Mallord William Turner: 1775-1851
Rogier van der Weyden: 1399 or 1400–1464
Rembrandt van Ryun: 1606–1669
Vincent Willem van Gogh: 1853–1890
Domenico Veneziano: c. 1410–1461

Acknowledgments:

The author and the Press thank the editors in whose journals some of these poems appeared, some in earlier versions and with different titles:

"Aide-Memoire": *The Flutes of Power*, Great Elm Press, 1995; *New to North America: Writing by Immigrants, Their Children & Grandchildren*, Abby Bogomolny, editor, Burning Bush Publications, 1997; The Great Blue Heron and Other Poems, Adrienne Lee Press 1997; as "Note to a Poet in Exile": PEN's Writers-in-Exile, 1988; *The Arc of the Storm*, Signal Books, © 1998 Elisavietta Ritchie;

"Amadeo Modigliani: *Adrienne (Woman with Bangs)*": *The Broadkill Review*, Vol. 6, No, 1; *From the Artist's Deathbed; Tiger Upstairs on Connecticut Avenue*, Cherry Grove Collections, © 2013;

"At Deadline, or, Pierre Bonnard: *The Letter*": *Innisfree*, Spring 2012; First Prize, Poetry Society of Georgia yearbook, 2011; *From the Artist's Deathbed*, a chapbook in anthology *Ashes Caught on the Edge of Light: Ten Chapbooks*, The Winterhawk Press, © 2012 Elisavietta Ritchie; *Tiger Upstairs on Connecticut Avenue*, Cherry Grove Collections,
© Elisavietta Ritchie 2013;

"Auguste Renoir: *Lady with a Parasol in a Garden*": *The Broadkill Review*, Vol. 6, No, 1; *From the Artist's Deathbed; Tiger Upstairs on Connecticut Avenue;*

"Camille Pissarro: *The Bather* Speaks": *The Ledge*, winner The Poetry Prize, 2012; *From the Artist's Deathbed; Tiger Upstairs on Connecticut Avenue;*

Anonymous American: *Cat and Kittens* as "That Feline Need," *The Broadkill Review*, Vol. 4, No. 2, 2010;

John James Audubon: *Snowy Egret* as "In the Canal beyond Newark, New Jersey," *Concise* 2009; *Little Patuxent Review*, 2009; *Feathers, Or, Love on the Wing*, Shelden Studios, © 2012 Elisavietta Ritchie, Megan Richard, Suzanne Shelden; *Cormorant Beyond the Compost*, Cherry Grove Collections, © 2011 Elisavietta Ritchie;

Pierre Bonnard: *The Letter* as "Admonition to Myself Not to Waste My Time," *The Broadkill Review*, 2009; *Tiger Upstairs on Connecticut Avenue;*

"Pierre Bonnard: *Her Children*": *Spillway*, December 2010; *Tiger Upstairs on Connecticut Avenue;*

Paul Cezanne: *Man with Pipe*, as "He Only Smoked a Pipe," accepted for an unrealized anthology *K.I.S.S. Your Butts Goodbye*, editor George J. Pearce III, 2006;

Richard Chew: *Lobster, Conanicut Island, Narragansett Bay*, as "For a Certain Artist," as inspired by Marsden Hartley's *Lobster on Black Background* and Yasuo Kuniyoshi's *The Swimmer; Folio* 2000; *Tiger Upstairs on Connecticut Avenue;*

Edgar Degas: *Woman Ironing*, as "Sorting Laundry," *Poetry* ©1988, Modern Poetry Society; *Sound and Sense*, 8th edition, Perrine and Arp, editors, Harcourt Brace Jovanovich Inc. 1991; *Sound and Sense* 11th edition; *Perrine's Literature: Structure, Sound and Sense*, 9th edition, Heinle & Heinle Publishers, 2004; *Perrine's Literature,* Arp & Johnson, Heinle/Arts and Sciences, Edition 11, 2011, Cengage Learning Inc./Nelson Education Ltd, ISBN 978044958965; *A Wound-Up Cat and Other Bedtime Stories,* Palmerston Press, ©1993 Elisavietta Ritchie; *The Arc of the Storm*, Signal Books, © 1998 Elisavietta Ritchie; prose version in *Flying Time: Stories & Half- Stories*, Signal Books, ©1992 & 1996 Elisavietta Ritchie; *Love Over 60: an anthology of women's poems*, editors Robin Chapman and Jeri McCormick, Mayapple Press, 2010; and on various Internet sites;

Albrecht Durer: *St. Jerome and his Lion*: as "House Lions," *Blue Unicorn*, 2004; *The Spirit of the*

Walrus, Bright Hill Press, 2005; *Awaiting Permission to Land* winner of the Anamnesis Award), Cherry Grove Collections, © 2006, Elisavietta Ritchie;

"Marsden Hartley: *Canuck Yankee Lumberjack at Old Orchard Beach, Maine,"* *Potomac Review,* 2000; Catalogue for *The Old New England Exhibit,* National Museum of American Art;

Marie Laurencin: *Girl and a Dove*: as "Dialogue with Mourning Dove," *The Broadkill Review,* 2010; *Cormorant Beyond the Compost;*

Edouard Manet: *At the Races* as "My Race Horses," *The Broadkill Review*, Vol. 3 No. 2, 2009; *Cormorant Beyond the Compost;* "Mesimaria," *A Sheaf of Dreams and Other Games, "*Proteus Press, 1976;

Zivko Milic: *The Yellow Car*: *Visions International,* 2010*; Cormorant Beyond the Compost;*

Pablo Picasso: *Petrus Manach*: as "Can't You See I'm Working?" *The Broadkill Review*, 2009; "The Artist's Wife Speaks:" part 1, as "Can't You Tell I'm Working?" *The Broadkill Review,* 2009; part 2, as "Camille Pissarro's *Artist's Garden at Eragny*: The Artist's Wife Speaks:" *The Broadkill Review,* Vol. 6, No, 1; *From the Artist's Deathbed; Tiger Upstairs on Connecticut Avenue;*

"Pablo Picasso: *Tragedy*": *The Innisfree Poetry Journal,* 2012; *Tiger Upstairs on Connecticut Avenue;*

"Camille Pissarro: *The Bather*": First Prize, *The Ledge,* 2011 Poetry Award, in print Spring, 2012; *Tiger Upstairs on Connecticut Avenue; The Art of Survival: an anthology,* Kings Estate Press, in-press, editor Ruth Moon Kempher, 2014;

Auguste Renoir: *Odalisque: Algerienne Reclining,* as "The Gypsy Appears Before the Commandant," *Whose Woods These Are; Finding The Name, 1986; Tiger Upstairs on Connecticut Avenue;*

Megan Richard: *Moony Night*: as "Lunatic Moons" in *Guy Wires,* ©2015 Poets' Choice Publishing;

Henri de Toulouse Lautrec: *Yvette Guilbert, diseuse / storyteller,* as "Advice Column" and as "Old Flame, or Portrait of a Woman of Action," *Pulpsmith; Lite Year '86; A Wound-Up Cat and Other Bedtime Stories,* Palmerston Press, © 1993 Elisavietta Ritchie; *Singles Magazine* 1993; Prose version in *Flying Time: Stories and Half-Stories,* Signal Books, © Elisavietta Ritchie; 1992 Elisavietta Ritchie;

Rogier van der Weyden: *Portrait of a Lady as* "Tradecraft in Iambic Pentameters: For a child who doubts I can keep secrets," *The Broadkill Review,* 2010; *Cormorant Beyond the Compost*;

Henri de Toulouse Lautrec: *Yvette Guilbert, diseuse / storyteller,* as "Advice Column" and as "Old Flame, or Portrait of a Woman of Action," *Pulpsmith; Lite Year '86; A Wound-Up Cat and Other Bedtime Stories,* Palmerston Press, © 1993 Elisavietta Ritchie; *Singles Magazine* 1993; Prose version in *Flying Time: Stories and Half-Stories,* Signal Books, © Elisavietta Ritchie; 1992 Elisavietta Ritchie;

Rogier van der Weyden: *Portrait of a Lady as* "Tradecraft in Iambic Pentameters: For a child who doubts I can keep secrets," *The Broadkill Review,* 2010; *Cormorant Beyond the Compost*;

"When Foxes Came Calling": *The Bay Weekly, September 15-21, 2016.*

Biographical Note on Author

Elisavietta Ritchie's prose, poetry, photographs, translations are widely published, translated, and anthologized in the United States and abroad. Credits include *New York Times, Washington Post, Poetry, American Scholar, Christian Science Monitor, JAMA: Journal of the American Medical Association, Canadian Woman Studies, Confrontation, Potomac Review,* numerous other publications.

Certain Russian artists and poets, such as Osip Mandelstam, Kornei Chukovsky and Samuel Marshak, who in the especially dour 1930s in the USSR were not free to paint and write as they wished, to make a living wrote and illustrated books for children. All her Aunt Maria Leonidovna was allowed to send from Leningrad, these inspired Ritchie's haiku-like poems in Russian and English age three. As a graduate teaching fellow at American University many years later, in her imperfect Russian she wrote a mini-thesis on the dissident artists in the USSR in the 1960s, and later hosted several who managed to emigrate. Professor Boris Filipov also told her to write another thesis comparing Anna Akhmatova's early and later love poems.

Tightening The Circle Over Eel Country won the Great Lakes Colleges Association's "New Writer's Award, 1975-1976." Individual poems and stories won significant awards from the Poetry Society of America, National Endowment for the Arts, *The Ledge,* Bright Hill Press, and others. Several were nominated for the Pushcart Prize.

Ritchie writes, translates, edits, gives readings, workshops, serves as poet-in-the-schools, helps writers of various ages, and has long been active with both the poetry and fiction divisions of Washington Writers' Publishing House, where, after winning annual awards for a book of poetry then of fiction, she served first as president of the poetry then the fiction division. She traveled to several continents independently and as a Visiting Overseas Speaker for the United States Information Service. She has since presented several Powerpoint talks of many of these poems with the paintings which inspired them.

Ritchie has been nurturing poets, painters, musicians and wildlife, and writing on the shores of the Patuxent River, Maryland, the Potomac, Washington DC, and rivers and seacoasts of Cyprus, Malaysia, the Balkans, Australia, Canada and briefly, the USSR and the African continent. The cover photos show the cove she and her writer husband Clyde Farnsworth see as they write. The old farmhouse (during Prohibition belonging to bootlegger George Banning) resembles a Russian *dacha*. She herself has never managed to paint more than rooms and boats.

www.ingramcontent.com/pod-product-compliance
Lightning Source LLC
Chambersburg PA
CBHW061928290426
44113CB00024B/2846